MAKE ROOM FOR BLOOMS

By Jackie Trainor
illustrated by Kerrie McNeill

Text Copyright © Jackie Trainor
Illustrations Copyright © Kerrie McNeill

All rights reserved. No part of this publication may be reproduced, or transmitted in any form, or by any means, electrical, mechanical, photocopying, recording or otherwise without the written permission of the publishers.

ISBN # 979-8-218-25300-4

Printed in the United States of America.

This Book Belongs To:

Iris steps out,
her head full of doubt.
Two feet at a time,
when she lets out a whine,
"I can't do it!
My stupid feet can't

jump or leap!

"Iris, what's wrong my dear?" inquired her mother.

"I just can't do it! I can't jump rope. I am not fit. I've lost all hope!"

Iris' Mom just smiled and said, "My little seed, you must make room for blooms!"

"Iris, pick a plant, take a seat.
Come now, move those feet."

Iris' mother calmly cared for the plant, "Every day, there is a new bloom, even when it feels like you've run out of room."

But when we tend to ourselves, we can mend."

"HOW FAST WILL IT GROW?

HOW WILL I KNOW?!"
Iris boomed.

"Be patient, my little seed.
Time is what you need."
her Mother whispered softly.

Iris heard her mother's words in her thoughts, *"Say kind words to yourself."*

"You are a strong plant! You will grow big and tall!"

"I am strong. I am smart." Iris says with her whole heart.

"Be sure to get plenty of light."

Iris knows that friends shouldn't always make you feel blue.

"Most importantly, remember, when it all feels too much...

When all feels lost..."

"Reach out to the ones who love you the most."

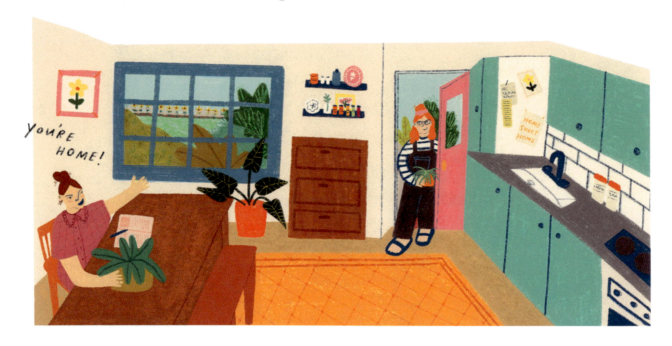

ALL deserve the room to bloom.

Some plants are prickly.

Some are looooong.

Some are colorful.

Some have flowers.

Some can heal.

Some have tangles.

Made in the USA
Middletown, DE
16 May 2024

54421304R00015